MARRIAGE COUNSELING

Simple Relationship Advice to Help Bring
Intimacy Back into Your Love Life

*** Two books in one – "How to Understand Men" and
"How to Understand Women" ***

HOW TO UNDERSTAND MEN

Emotional Availability, Attraction, and Getting Him to Obsess Over You

K. CONNORS

Table of Contents

INTRODUCTION

Do you find it difficult to understand your man? How do your conversations end? Doesn't he want you to want him to too? Or do you find it hard to do what he wants you to do? Yes, most women find it very challenging to understand men. Most women think men are more complicated than anything else in the world, thus leading to breakups.

It's funny how men find it difficult to understand women and women find it difficult to understand men. However, there are ways for these two individuals to meet halfway. Women can still understand what men think and what men say. You just simply need to learn how to read the clues and the signs. Once you do, your relationships will be better and stronger.

Men are not as difficult to understand as some might think. Read on and you will find useful tips to understand what men want to say and what men want you to do. Knowing how to understand men is one important thing that most women long for, but don't always succeed on the first try. Women sometimes have trouble with not being understood in relationships, but often neglect about how to understand men in their lives.

CHAPTER 1

HOW TO UNDERSTAND MEN

Knowing how to understand men is one important thing that women need to keep in mind. Women sometimes think of not being understood in a relationship - but often neglect about how to understand men in their lives. In the end, we sometimes find our spouses cheating on us and not understanding why. So early on, let us try to decipher what men really want from women.

WHY ARE MEN SO ENGROSSED WITH SEX?

Men's sexual drive is indeed different from that of a woman. The hormone testosterone in the man is responsible for wanting sex, as caused by their libido. Thus, it is but normal for men to be constantly looking for sex. If you want to understand men and their sex drives, you might also want to understand that they have different feelings towards sex because of the testosterone pressure they feel in their bodies. In relationships, many women seek attention; for love and pampering and men tend to be seeking for sex. Knowing these differences and understanding

3

why these differences exist, will truly help you in how to please your partner to make them happy in marriage.

MEN NEED SPACE FOR THEMSELVES

This goes the same for women as well. We all need space in our lives. Being in a relationship or tying the knot with the man you love does not necessarily mean clinging to that man day after day. Sometimes when women are so overwhelmed and in love, they tend to love having their man around and spending time with him, but need to understand that sometimes men want to have their quiet time or time with friends. Just because you are married, doesn't mean you always have to tag along with your man anywhere he goes. In marriage, you can manage this by giving time for him to be by himself and schedule time for you to spend together. Although too much space for both of you can also be bad for the relationship, so it is important to create balance.

MEN NEED TIME TO THINK

You may probably get upset when you are trying to bring up a concern and your man doesn't seem to respond to it immediately. Sometimes, women think men are not interested in what they regarding issues that are brought to their attention. To women, it seems like he may be thinking about something else, which sometimes can end up in an argument in itself. It is important to understand that most often, men want to process their problems and their thoughts to themselves, and they may want to think about it for some time. Oftentimes, men want to talk about it when they are able to come up with a solution, as opposed to talking about it piece by piece.

These are just three ways on how to understand men in your life. There are still a lot of differences between men and women that somehow we need to understand to help us build a good relationship with our significant other. So, the next time you get upset or angry, take the time to put yourself in their shoes and try to understand how they're thinking about it and their behavior towards the situation.

CHAPTER 2

WHAT THE MAJORITY OF MEN LOOK FOR IN WOMEN

When it comes to relationship issues, many men ajust aren't as savvy as women. When encountered with a problem, women will search for an answer be it through relationship manuals or advice columns, and even take advice from friends who also have relationship problems. Some men spend time protecting their egos rather than allowing themselves to be honest about what they really want in a relationship. In reality, deep down, men want the same things as the majority of wome. That is to find a lifelong partner, a soul mate, someone to love and be loved in return by a person who makes their hearts flutter uncontrollably. To have a long and happy life and to grow old with that special person. Men long to find a woman who can stimulate them romantically, emotionally and intellectually.

HERE ARE SOME OF THE QUALITIES A MAN LOOKS FOR IN A WOMAN.

Men are attracted to a woman who exudes both sensuality and femininity and who makes the imagination run wild. The male instinct is to look for all potential partners as long term mates and look for a woman they feel will be loyal and trustworthy.

Women love to be seduced and men are no different. Men like to think they are in charge and want a woman who can let them be strong, even after she is aware of their weaknesses. It is not in a man's psychological makeup to admit to not being able to handle any situation, so they need a woman who can make them stronger than they can be on their own.

One thing that is very common in men is fear of commitment. Men can go into battle to fight wars, swim with sharks or jump out of a plane, but the thought of being with one woman for the rest of our lives induces some kind of uncontrollable fear.

Men like having options. They might think they are ready to settle down with that special woman they just met, but still leave the possibility open that someone else may come along. However, when a man really does commit, then he will really love and cherish his woman.

Real men appreciate real women. To a man, that is a woman who is strong but who will still allow the man to lead (sometimes), someone who is intelligent but still willing to learn. Someone who understands them and their dreams and who is willing to help them achieve it. And finally, someone sensual, but is loyal and faithful.

It is important for a man to have a woman who contributes to the relationship and does not seek only what she can get out of it. In short, a man wants a feminine, sensual, trustworthy soul mate. This of course doesn't encompass 100% of the men out there, as there are always exceptions.

QUALITIES MEN LOOK FOR IN WOMEN

Asking what qualities men look for in women is a bit like asking what flavors of ice cream they like. Every man will be different, but there will always be a few obvious favorites. To some extent, the qualities men look for in women depend on what the man wants from their partner as they will look for different qualities in a marriage partner then they will for someone to have fun with on a Saturday night. Chocolate Brownie might be their ice cream of choice, but if you're asking them to eat a whole tub, maybe they'd prefer Butter Pecan? With that in mind, here are a few of the usual qualities men look for in women.

We have to start with physical qualities because there's no denying that the initial attraction a man feels towards a woman is likely to be physical. You might be surprised what men find physically attractive. The media would have us believe that men only go for skinny, leggy blondes with enormous breasts, but how many men do you know that have actually ended up with girls like that? An average looking woman that smiles or laughs a lot is generally more attractive to a man than a natural beauty who is permanently sulking or scowling. Finding a style that suits you and accentuates your good points, rather than trying to be something you are not, will make you look great and will increase your confidence; a trait that men find very appealing. Ladies, true beauty lies within your confidence.

Men do appreciate it when women make an effort with their appearance. This doesn't mean you need to cake on the makeup, but if it brings out your good features, knock yourself out. However, worrying about your hairstyle or new shoes getting messed up can stop you from being any fun and that is a real turn off.

Independence can be an attractive quality for some men. Having your own interests and friends, as well as your own ideas and views, can make a woman more interesting to be around. Financial independence is a tricky one, however. If they are entirely honest, a lot of men can't cope with their woman earning more than they do. It's just the traditional ideology that's getting more and more outdated. I say make as much money as you can; men that are threatened by this frankly need to get over it.

To continue with the 1950s stereotype, it is true that men do like to be looked after. Being able to cook a half decent meal, iron his shirts and look after his kids, is something that a man will be looking for in a woman. This may sound old fashioned in the twenty-first century, but that doesn't stop it from being true. Desperation is a really unattractive trait in a woman, so no matter how much you like a guy, or want to get married and have babies, for heaven's sake play it cool. You need to let him know you're interested, but listening to his stories and smiling at him is more effective than stalking him after the first date, or declaring your undying love. Surprisingly, the majority of men are looking to find a partner they can settle down with, but start talking marriage and children and you're in danger of scaring him off. Some men enjoy the chase, while others don't. I prefer the route of being up front, and don't make either one of you do most of the running.

Overall, men are looking for women that are cheerful, positive, and fun to be around. No guy is going to stick around for long if you are constantly complaining, even if you do look like a supermodel. Being adventurous and willing to try new things is a very attractive quality, but don't be scared to be a little weak or vulnerable, most men like to feel they can protect their women. You may feel that no man will ever find you attractive, but consider a few of these simple rules and you'll be fighting off the admirers.

CHAPTER 3

WHAT IS ATTRACTIVE TO MOST MEN?

What is attractive to men? That's the one question every woman wishes she knew the answer to. Some women struggle with understanding exactly how to appeal to the guy they're interested in. They take our cues from what they see around them and that's not always the best path to take, however logical it may seem. If you try and transform yourself into what you think he wants, based on what the media is suggesting men want, you may find yourself alone and confused. There are specific qualities that men are naturally drawn to within a woman. Focus on these and he'll be chasing after you in no time.

HERE ARE QUALITIES THAT MEN FIND IRRESISTIBLE IN A WOMAN:

1. A SENSE OF HUMOR: Men want to have fun and they love to laugh. They long to be with someone who doesn't take life too seriously and who is willing to laugh at the world around her and herself. Find your sense of humor and embrace it. He'll love being around you if you always

make him smile. You don't have to be a comedian, just show that you love life and love to have a good time. Smiling and laughing is one of the best ways to show this.

2. SELF-ACCEPTANCE: You'll never be perfect. None of us ever will be. That's just a fact of life. If you want to make yourself attractive to a particular man, just accept the woman you are, flaws and all. If you're not constantly making excuses for the way you look, your attitude or what you do for a living, he'll find that very appealing. Men are used to interacting with women who try and excuse away their shortcomings. Don't do that!

3. GENUINE COMPASSION: To most men, one quality that an ideal woman will always possess is compassion. They envision their future partner to have a heart of gold and to always put others before themself. Be kind to everyone, every day. Not only will this show him that you're a genuinely good person, it will make you feel great about yourself too.

4. HONESTY: You may think that you can get away with telling a white lie to your guy but you won't. Men can see through a false front in no time, whether they reveal it or not. He wants to know that he can always trust you and that means that you have to be honest with him 100% of the time.

5. THE SENSE OF ADVENTURE: No, this doesn't mean that you have to be willing to go skydiving with him. But

you should be open to the idea of a fun and interesting adventure from time-to-time. If you're not one for spur of the moment change, you may actually turn him off. Men crave to be with someone who is ready to jump in the car at a moment's notice and go explore parts unknown. Show him that spontaneity is your middle name and he'll want to spend as much time with you as he can. Always ensure your best qualities shine through when you are trying to win the attention and adoration of a special man. If you push aside all those self-doubts, the real you will shine through and he won't be able to resist you.

CHAPTER 4

THE FIRST DATE, WHAT TO EXPECT OR DO

So Prince Charming has finally asked you out. You've been desperately trying to get his attention. You finally did and now you have a date planned. You're so excited that you can hardly stand it. Then come the flood of questions that run through your mind. What am I going to wear? What should I do with my hair? Where will we go? What will we do?

And then comes the biggest one of all... what are we going to talk about? Did you know that one of the most important first date tips for women involves the conversation and what you talk about during the date? It's true and the reason is because it is what captures a man's attention most. Don't get me wrong. You do want to look good, even hot. But your looks will only take you so far as to get the first date. From there, it's what you say that will leave him wanting more. Now the question becomes, "What can I say to nail the first date and clinch a second?" This is the dating advice you really need, so pay close attention.

First dates can never be forgotten, you will remember your first date throughout your whole life. At first, first dates can really build up a sweat in you. You could be shy and not talk much which could also be reasons why your second date with the same person might never take off. On the other hand, you could be really talkative and not let the other speak, over confident, etc., which is not what the other person might expect. This could be another reason why you could blow up your first date. If you want to make sure that your first date is not only memorable, but lands you the chance on a second one, then there are a few pointers that you might want to consider. Although these are not foolproof, they will surely give you the right amount of confidence and you will be your perfect best.

1. CLEAN UP

Make sure that you take a bath or shower and don't forget to spray up some perfume or cologne. It is important that you are clean and smell decent too. Guys need to make sure they don't turn up unshaven or looking frumpy. Women, don't look ratchet. You don't want to look messy on your first date. The first impression is the last impression in this case.

2. WHERE TO GO?

Suggest to your partner that you have your date in a restaurant, a movie theater, picnic area, or any venue where there are other people around. This way, your date cannot get too cozy with you. Spending time together where you are given too much privacy is not a good idea to spend your first date. As a woman, you need to think of your safety first. It's also good to participate in an ongoing activity like bowling, miniature golf, etc., as awkward silences are almost inevitable in a stagnant environment.

3. WHAT TO WEAR?

Do not wear provocative clothing as you will be sending the wrong message to your date. This does not mean that you should wear "granny" clothes to show that you are a conservative type. The point is to dress attractively, not promiscuously.

4. WHAT TO TALK ABOUT?

Most men expect women to start the conversation first. Whether you like it or not, this is just how it is. If your date is the quiet type, then you may feel pressured to keep talking just so avoid deafening silence. But make sure that you strike an intelligent conversation. Do not just babble about anything and everything under the sun. First date tips for women would tell you not to monopolize the conversation. Do not talk too much about yourself. Give him a chance to talk about himself as well.

5. BE INTERESTING

This does not mean you hog up the entire conversation and talk about yourself all the time. First dates are a great time to know if you've made the right choice; it's the time for meaningful conversations where you get to know each other's likes and dislikes. Don't steal the limelight and talk about yourself unless asked. Make sure that you give your date a chance to talk about themselves too. Get to know everything that is relevant like hobbies, favorites, family, etc. This will keep the conversation interesting and you will have a wonderful time. In fact, this is just the tip of the iceberg, and you will unknowingly pave the way for a second date.

6. BE THERE ON TIME

Just like an interview (this is essentially what a first date is), it is important that you turn up for your first date on time or else you will only send out the wrong signal. Make sure that you inform your date in case you are held up somewhere and it could take you some time to get there, that way your date won't feel abandoned. Women love to keep their men waiting, it's best that you don't overdo it though, a few minutes late is understandable, but nothing beyond that.

7. CHOOSE AN ACTIVITY YOU ENJOY

On the first date, you should choose an activity that you honestly enjoy. If you choose an activity that you hate, but you think your date will enjoy, your body language may give up the ruse you are trying to pull. However, if you do something you like, your attitude will be great without you having to worry about it.

TIPS FOR WOMEN ON HOW TO LOOK YOUR BEST ON YOUR FIRST DATE

When it comes to first dates, appearance matters. The way you dress and present yourself to your date will speak volumes about your character, whether the conversation is flowing freely or not. This is equally true for both men and women, and the first impressions your date gleans from your appearance may make the difference between a second date and a brush-off. When you meet someone for the first time, you no doubt pay close attention to his or her appearance, whether consciously or sub-consciously. This includes things like clothing, hairstyle, and odor, and in the absence of much other information about the person sitting across from us, these little clues are what we go on to assess their suitability as a potential partner. Needless to say, whilst you sit there quietly judging this perfect or not so perfect stranger, your date is doing the same.

So what can you do to ensure that your appearance makes for a favorable first impression on your date?

1. MAKE-UP- LESS IS MORE

Most men like a woman who looks good with make-up on, but they also want to know that when the makeup comes off, what's underneath is just as appealing. Wearing too much make-up also runs the risk of ruining the skin underneath and may indicate to your date that you're a little lax in your skincare routine.

2. SKIN

A good skin care regime is important in maintaining skin that is soft to the touch and pleasant on the eye. As well as having a good diet and avoiding excessive amounts of time in direct sunlight, using anti-aging creams, anti-wrinkle lotions and moisturizers can do wonders for your skin. If you suffer from any skin conditions, visit your local GP to see if he or she can prescribe anything or offer advice.

3. HAIR

If you're going to get a haircut specifically for your date, go for a style you feel comfortable with, rather than one from a magazine that you think men will like. The most important thing is to feel that you can be yourself around your date, and this may be hard if you're wearing a Brazillian style cut. If you suffer at all from facial hair, consider trying laser hair removal treatments. Mustaches seldom look sexy on men (with a few exceptions), and even worse for women.

4. CLOTHES

Once again, wear clothes that you feel comfortable wearing, both physically and emotionally. Most men enjoy the sight of a woman wearing a killer dress, but it is also the confidence with which she carries herself that can make all the difference. If you're happy wearing something low-cut, then be bold and go for it. If you'd feel more comfortable in something a little more conservative then wear that instead.

5. SHOES

This last tip may fall on deaf ears, but men don't care that much about shoes and would prefer you to be comfortable in a pair of sensible yet attractive shoes rather than in constant pain caused by 'killer heels'. Try to find a balance between aesthetic beauty and practicality.

Here's one problem that most women face when they're about to go out with an attractive guy: What to wear. Why is this an issue? Women, in general, think that they will get judged by the way they dress. They also want to give the best first impression possible. For these reasons, women agonize over their choice of clothes and accessories for hours before deciding on one outfit that best represents their true personality and good taste. Be confident in what you wear. Dress comfortably, but attractive, and don't spend so much time on your shoes, because I can assure you your date could care less.

CHAPTER 5

WHY IT'S OBVIOUS WHEN A GUY LIKES YOU

If you have ever thought if a guy you are interested in likes you at all, you are not alone. If you knew just a few behavioral tendencies, you might notice this in advance and you could come up with a complimenting strategy. In the end, I will give you one easy and practical way to test this theory.

EYE-CONTACT

Start observing how he looks at you. If you didn't know him before, he might be staring at you from a distance. And every time he notices that you look at him, he turns away. Men stare without making eye contact because they like what they see, but lack the confidence to speak up.

Commonly known - "the look" - when the guy sweeps his eyes from your head to your toes with a slight tentative smile, this obviously means that he is interested. Unfortunately, it may also mean he's just looking to get laid. Of course, if that is what you also want - go for it! But if you want something deeper - be careful.

If you already know him, it is easier to make eye-contact with him. It's said that a woman can read a man's heart through his eyes and no man can disguise his feelings if you make straight eye-contact with him. A guy who likes you will also try to make eye-contact with you.

BODY LANGUAGE

You can also notice which way the guy is standing when he is watching you or talking to you. Just check which way his feet are pointing. If both of his feet are pointing towards you, it means that he is comfortable with that direction and does not need to have an escape route. His could be a good indication that he might like you.

FRIENDS

Men don't usually tell you straight if they like you or not. However, if they are interested they will tell their best friends that they would like to know more about you. They might even get their friends on board to find out more about you. If you notice this happening, it is a sure sign.

CONVERSATION

When you get the chance to talk to him it is much easier to find out whether he likes you or not. If he can be relaxed and just himself when you are around, that means he's comfortable with you. If this doesn't mean anything else, then at least you can good friends. On the other hand, if he is instead looking away or not paying attention to what you say, and you get the feeling that he would rather be somewhere else – you're most likely right. A shy guy (and also not so shy if he has a crush on you) would be nervous and cannot always be so natural when talking to a woman. If he is interested he will still try make eye-contact, smile and talk about the things you are interested in.

If a guy likes you he also shows interest in things you like and do. My advice is that you try to get a conversation to an area you like and feel comfortable to talk about. For example, if you like cats, don't hesitate to say that. It doesn't matter if the guy doesn't like cats at all - he might just start comparing them to dogs (which means he has paid attention to what you have said and is interested in your point of view). Remember to listen also to what he has to say and let him talk!

BEHAVIOR

How does the guy treat you? Many guys (not all) playfully tease a girl they like. He might also be more polite to you than the other girls. He opens your door, takes your coat, gives you a chair, etc. Any behavior that is different to you than the others means that there is something special. This different behavior is an easy and good sign.

TESTING

One easy and practical way to test if he really is interested is just take an innocent step inside his personal space. If he steps away, he is not interested or he is a really shy person. If he is interested, he will set the boundaries of his personal space closer for you and will allow you to come closer than normal.

HERE ARE OTHER SIGNS THAT A GUY LIKES YOU

1. HE HANGS AROUND A LOT

When a guy always seems to hang around you and tends to gravitate back towards you when you move away, you have a fairly good indication that he likes you. Guys that like you will make the most of every opportunity to be with you. They will also make a habit of popping up at places and events where they know you are going to be.

2. HE MAKES AN EFFORT TO CONVERSE WITH YOU

If some random guy makes a comment to you (e.g. "Nice day, isn't it?") or comes over and starts a conversation with you, then this is a clear sign that he likes you or is at least interested in getting to know you. Yes, he may have a very plausible reason to talk to a stranger, such as wanting to know the time or needing directions, but you won't know until you continue the conversation.

This can also be a sign that a guy likes you if the guy is someone that you know, but not that well. For example, a guy who works on the same floor as you comes over and says "Hi" when you are at the coffee machine.

3. HE SEEMS NERVOUS AROUND YOU

For some reason when a guy likes you, he will often act all weird and isn't able to be himself. He will likely appear very nervous when he is around you. The most common sign of this is that he will smile too much and may even make weird comments. Other signs are that he might stutter, blush, or have trouble maintaining eye contact with you.

4. HE TRIES REALLY HARD TO KEEP A CONVERSATION WITH YOU GOING

When a guy likes you, he will usually take personal responsibility to keep a conversation with you going. As the conversational thread starts to die, he will tend to quickly try and save it, or even start a new thread before the dreaded awkward silence occurs.

5. HE TOUCHES YOU WITH HIS HAND AS HE IS TALKING

As a guy is talking to you, he might touch you on the back or shoulder with his hand, as he emphasizes a point. He may even stroke your hair briefly. You can interpret these as attempts by him to be a bit flirtatious with you, as it is not usually appropriate to touch someone like this unless you are romantically involved with them.

6. HE FLIRTS WITH YOU

There are many different ways that a guy can flirt with you. He might do it in a very subtle way, such as touching you on the shoulder as he is talking, like I mentioned above. Other forms of flirting include: smiling at you, teasing you, or yes, even making fun of you from time to time.

7. YOU RECEIVE A FACEBOOK FRIEND REQUEST FROM HIM, WHEN YOU DON'T KNOW HIM THAT WELL

This can be a fairly reliable sign if the guy has no mutual Facebook friends with you and would have had to do a lot of searching to find your profile. But it is a less reliable sign if he has a number of Facebook friends in common with you. This is because Facebook keeps firing friend suggestions at people, who are actually our friends' friends. Furthermore, a lot of people on Facebook try to add anyone they can to up their friend count.

So now you know what things you need to pay attention for to figure out if the guy likes you: the look, body language, their friends and how he pays attention to your interests and how he treats you. Don't stress over these things; pick one or two to keep an eye out for, and see what comes along.

CHAPTER 6

WHY IS HE EMOTIONALLY UNAVAILABLE?

Trying to have a relationship with an emotionally unavailable man can be very frustrating. Contrary to popular belief, just because someone is single does not mean they are emotionally available for a relationship. Just because someone is single does not mean they are relationship ready. Not everyone will be searching for their soul mate, or romantic partner, or even at all during this lifetime. They may very well be in a different place than you in their journey and truly may only be seeking a casual relationship.

There are also people that have absolutely no intention of being monogamous (even though they lie and say they are) who will simply never be emotionally available for you. There are many reasons why people will not be emotionally available for the type of relationship you are looking for. It is not always easy to spot an emotionally unavailable man.

He may very well present himself to you in such a way that it makes you believe he is ready for love. Everything may even be progressing along nicely. You are spending time together and he may very well be pursuing you... and you like it. You have been hesitant with your feelings and are keeping them in check, but he has insisted that you are the best thing ever. He may even talk about the connection the two of you share. When you finally give in and allow yourself to have an emotional connection to him, out come the signals of the unavailability.. he withdraws, he pulls back, he starts to cancel dates or fails to respond to calls or messages. You are more confused than ever because he was the one who displayed the signs of being open emotionally.. but the instant you open up to him, the walls go up and the lines of communication go down. When the possibility of a real relationship became a reality to him, it was more than he could deal with… emotionally. As long as it was an idea, it was OK, but the reality of it caused him to bolt.

Before you let your heart invest in a relationship, you need to make sure the man you choose is emotionally available.

SIGNS OF EMOTIONALLY UNAVAILABLE MEN

1. Over-involvement in a career or in other people's lives. You want a man who has a purpose and reason for waking up each morning. He should ideally have a career that he enjoys and people who love and care about him. But too much involvement will be seen in that:

   a. His career is all that he talks and thinks about: One of the signs of an emotionally unavailable man is that all he talks about is his career; his only interest is his career; he excels only in his career, and he has no other interest in life apart from his career. If you observe him carefully, you will realize that the only thing that he truly loves is his.. wait for it.. CAREER. In all practical ways, he is in love and married to his job. He may want you in his life so that you can meet those needs that his job does not, but his true love and the one that holds his emotions is his job. He breathes, sleep, dreams and fantasizes about his career; and you will always be a lower emotional priority in his life.

b. He is everyone's go-to guy: Yes you want a man who has friends and is involved in their lives, but one of the signs of emotionally unavailable men is their insatiable need to serve their friends and family members in every single little thing. It may seem like a cute trait at the beginning of the relationship when you think that he is one of the most giving men that you know, but it could be a sign of emotional unavailability. If he is at the beck and call of all his friends and relatives, then he will have minimal or no time for you. He simply does not have the time to be emotionally available to you. You may resent his friends or family members, but the problem may be him...not his friends or family members.

2. He has huge personal baggage: We all have baggage from our pasts. Nobody is spared from the hurt we can receive from others. But emotionally unavailable men have the

type of baggage that cripples them emotionally. Whatever the past relationships did or did not do to them; emotionally unavailable men will react and treat you like the person or persons who hurt them in their past. He simply does not give you a chance to connect emotionally with him as he can only see you through the lenses of his past hurt.

3. He is just unable (or unwilling) to see the real you and so he creates (or sees) reasons why you are just like the people or person that hurt him in the past; and he disengages emotionally from you, ensuring that he can never be available to you when you need him to be. Some women find such men an irresistible challenge; they want to be the one that saves such a man and gets him to love again. But if you are one of those women then remember to tread carefully as this is a road full of incredible hurts and unless the man wants to change...all the love in the world may not be the proper course of action for them.

4. He has no real desire to be around you. A man who is emotionally unavailable also tends to be physically unavailable all the time. He may be in the same room or even sitting right next to you on the couch but his hands, eyes, and body never engage with you. He may go through the motions of living like eating; answer your questions with single answers or one liner's; have sex and do whatever you ask when at home. But he will not have any real interest in you and he will not cuddle, or hug you

or touch you lightly as he talks. His interaction with you gives you the eerie feeling that he is thousands or even million of miles away from you, even when he is sitting or lying right next to you.

5. He has no interest in the things that are uniquely you are on issues that concern you. A man that is emotionally unavailable is living on autopilot, much like a robot. He functions by doing the minimal that he can in his relationship with you. He is not truly interested in your life and its unique twists and turns or in the things that you want him to do. He may get involved if you harass and nag him into action but generally, it is an uphill battle getting him involved in 'your' things. He may respond when you tell him about your day, but if you pay attention to him, his body and replies, you can almost hear them screaming their total disinterest in all that concerns you.

6. Your conversations are confined to the mundane life stuff. When a man is emotionally unavailable to you he talks to you about non-issues. He talks only when he must and he does not talk about himself or the things that are dear to his heart and life. Instead, he will talk about the weather, the traffic or other such life stuff; and how it was, without telling you how it affected him or made him feel. He will talk like one who is an outside observer of his life.

His lack of emotional connection with you will make his conversation more like a commentary... like it happened, but not to him as he has no feelings about it that he cares enough to share with you.

7. Nothing about you and your life together gives him joy and happiness anymore (or so it seems that way). An emotionally unavailable man will not find you a source of pleasure. He may not be completely unhappy, but episodes of sheer delight and pleasure with you will be rare or non-existent... and you will know it.

8. He is an emotionally dead man only when he is around you: A man that is emotionally unavailable to you will display this action only when around you. When he is around other people he will be animated and engaged, and he will actually seem like a different man entirely. He will be passionate, engaged and happy around them. Do not believe the lie that it is because he has a passion for football or he has known the other people longer, etc. The truth is that he is not emotionally available to you.

These signs in combination with your intuition will let you know whether or not your man is emotionally unavailable to you. When you know that your man is emotionally unavailable, the next stage will be understood as to why he is disconnected from you. He may be going through a life crisis or he may just want out of the relationship.

Whichever the reson may be, it is imperative that you try your best not to take it personally. It may just be that he wans't ready for a commitment. Yea, it hurts, but this type of negative thinking will only create backage and worry. This type of baggage can be carried on into your next relationship, and possibly ruin what could be a good thing. If this happens to you, understand that you are not alone and that it may not even be a reflection of you. Some individuals need to work on themselves before they can enjoy the company of others in a committed relationship.

SO WHAT CAN YOU DO?

The simplest and most clear answer to this is to distance yourself. But this is not easy to do for the majority of women out there, as some women feel that they can logically convince the guy to open up emotionally. This is just not possible for most, or at least sustainable for long periods of time.Therefore, it's very important for you to leave him alone and draw a line. If you don't let him know that you're not okay with him not being emotionally available to you right away, then you are only dragging things further which will lead to nothing but pain for both of you.

Infact, the major reason why you must draw the line and leave him alone for the time being is because once he knows that you are not okay with his actions, he will either change himself completely for you or you will finally know that he's just not someone you can spend the rest of your life with.

Emotionally unavailable men can turn your life upside down if you make the mistake of continuing to entertain the thought of being with them. They may present a challenge to some women or elevate the caring intuition in other women, but whatever emotions they evoke in you; know with certainty that loving them will be a journey to relationship hurts and heartbreaks.

CHAPTER 7

HEALTHY RELATIONSHIPS, NOT RELATIONSHITS.

There are many people whose preference is to have healthy relationships with the people in their lives; whether they are parent-child relationships, marriage or love relationships, family relationships, friendships, or even relationships with work colleagues. Building healthy relationships is a normal and natural desire. In fact, healthy relationships are a vital aspect of mental health, general health and wellness. So what do we need to know about building and maintaining healthy relationships?

Let us define some of the qualities of healthy relationships:

Each person takes responsibility for their own needs

You can easily discuss conflict and differences, without blame

The relationship is important to each person involved

Each person communicates openly and honestly

Abuse is absent; this includes physical, verbal, and emotional abuse

Each person has healthy boundaries -- can say "no" to requests without feelings of guilt

Certainly, it is important for each party in a relationship to understand, and be able to practice these aspects when interacting with others. It is my belief, however, that the key to healthy relationships is found, first, in our interactions with our Self, with our Inner Being.

What is your relationship like with your Inner Being?

Are you in conflict with yourself?

Do you ever bring blame on yourself?

Do you get angry or frustrated with yourself?

Is your relationship with your Inner Being important to you?

Do you communicate openly and honestly with your Inner Being?

Do you abuse yourself; physically or with thoughts or words?

Can you follow your inner guidance without feeling guilty?

If your relationship with your Inner Being is not a healthy one, then keeping up a healthy relationship with others in your life could be challenging for you. The relationship you have with your Inner Being is the most important relationship you will ever have, and every other relationship is a reflection (in some way) of that most intimate, inner one.

Do you ever feel angry or frustrated with yourself, or blame and criticize yourself? Your Inner Being never argues with you, or blames you, or gets angry or frustrated or disappointed with you... your Inner Being always beams pure, positive, love and energy to you -- without exception. If you blame or criticize yourself, then you are in conflict with your Inner Being -- and you feel that tension through negative emotions.

Do you value your relationship with your Inner Being? Is it important to you to feel good and feel happy? When you value your relationship with your Inner Being, then you make every effort you can to feel happy, and to focus your attention on thoughts that feel good when you think them.

Do you communicate honestly and openly with your Inner Being? This is as easy as tuning into your emotions. Your emotions give you feedback about your relationship with your Inner Being...when you feel positive, happy emotions, you are in tune with youself. Negative emotions show that you are thinking of something that does not agree with what your Inner Being knows.

Do you take the time to nurture your relationship with your Inner Being? Do you nurture and soothe yourself? There are many ways you can nurture your spirit...you can meditate or listen to soothing music. You can also nurture yourself by thinking of someone you love, by taking a warm bath, by taking a walk, or by just giving yourself permission to chill... even if just for a moment.

Do you abuse yourself physically or with thoughts or words? It always feels good to receive support and encouragement from others...but we can also be supportive and encouraging toward ourselves. This can mean not asking or demanding too much of ourselves in time and effort -- by realizing that you don't have to do whatever-it-is this minute. We can applaud our efforts, and focus on what we did right (and not what went wrong).

HOW TO MAINTAIN A HEALTHY RELATIONSHIP

Maintaining a healthy relationship is key in the light of breakups and separation, which occurs frequently between boyfriends, girlfriends, and lovers; divorce, lawsuits, and issues with regard to single parenting that occurs between Spouses, Couples or partners is quickly becoming a growing concern among individuals and young couples. All those who are in troubled marriages or are in crisis-ridden relationships and affairs must endeavor to return back to learn and master the art of creating and maintaining a healthy relationship today rather than just throwing in the towel, quit or give up on their once beautiful, lovely, romantic and resourceful relationship.

Creating a healthy relationship and maintaining it is a matter of choice. It is about how prepared both of you are and how committed you are to work things out when it gets tough. To get you started, here are a few thought provoking tips on how to maintain a healthy relationship:

1. ALWAYS BE YOURSELF

You are wonderfully and uniquely made. If you find that you have to act or try to become someone you weren't born to be, in order to fulfill someone else's expectations, then something is seriously wrong. A true love will appreciate you for who you are and what you bring to the relationship, and vice-versa. If you feel as if you're being pressured to alter your character to do things you wouldn't usually do (drink, drugs, premature sex, lie) so that the person will continue to see you, that's a certain sign that things are unhealthy. Your true love will gladly embrace you just for who you are; so don't be afraid, step out on faith and show your true self.

2. DEVELOP DEEP COMMUNICATION WITH EACH OTHER

A healthy relationship goes much deeper than a surface affair. Even though you may both look good arm-in-arm, or standing next to each other, whether at a concert, family reunion, movie theater, or at church, can you talk when you're alone? What's going on in your conversations? Are they deep and meaningful or surface and bland? Do you discuss personal hopes, dreams, and goals, or just talk about the weather and the plot of the latest drama? Can you count on each other to lend a listening ear, good advice, and undivided attention? Good, honest, and deep conversation will keep you deeply connected. When in doubt, talk it out. Always keep the lines of communication open in your relationship.

3. DON'T IGNORE, BUT EXPLORE YOUR DIFFERENCES

Do your personalities blend well? Is one of you on the optimistic path while the other is on the pessimistic side of the road? Opposites may initially attract, but eventually, they can repel each other. It's important that your personalities are compatible. If one views life through rose colored glasses, while the other is always singing-the-blues, then you have to make some sort of adjustment to accommodate each other. The simple truth is oil and vinegar make an excellent salad dressing, but they don't mix well in romantic relationships, unless both personalities can explore each other and find some sort of balance. If you can adjust and love each other's personality, regardless of any differences, and bring out the best when you're together, then this is a winning combo, and you could very well be a dynamic duo in a lifelong healthy relationship.

4. SHARE SIMILAR INTEREST AND VALUES

You don't have to have the same exact interests. As a matter of fact, having diverse preferences can help you to share new and exciting things with each other. However, make sure you have at least a few common interests, so it won't be an ongoing battle over what to do and where to go to keep you both satisfied. You may have to compromise in some areas like sports, politics, movies, shopping, music, etc. Keep in mind that compromising doesn't mean depriving each other of their individual interests, but instead it means participating in each other's interests.

5. DISCUSS YOUR SPIRITUAL BELIEFS TOGETHER

If you're not on the common ground with your beliefs about who and what God means to each of you (or lack of), this will eventually cause a rift in your relationship. Don't try to conceal your true beliefs and hope that it will all just one day fall into place; it won't. Make sure you talk about your faith honestly and openly with each other.

6. APPRECIATE EACH OTHER'S UNIQUE BODY TEMPLE

Let's face it, we're all built differently. We come in a variety of shapes, sizes, and shades. In order to have a healthy physical and emotional relationship, you must embrace and appreciate each other's total package. One of the worse things a couple can do to each other is to fantasize or try to fit their mate into someone else's body image. When you throw away the preconceived "ideal body type" perceptions, you'll enjoy the true worth of your partner.

7. TALK ABOUT SEX AND MONEY

Two of the biggest destroyers of healthy relationships are the misuse, abuse, lack of or over-use of sex and money. Both are very important and very personal in your love life. Yet, unfortunately, most couples make the mistake of not setting quality time aside early in their relationship to discuss these two vital components. To put it bluntly, "You've got to know where you're heading before you get to the bedding; and know what you're spending before it gets beyond mending."

In deep romantic relationships, there is a world of difference between "having sex" and "making love," just as there is a major difference between being "involved" and "being in love." The misuse of sex, just like the misuse of money, can cause major turbulence in a relationship. These can be dangerous influences which can overwhelm your relationship, or they can be healthy tools for intimacy and success. It's up to both you and your partner to know what sex and money mean to each of you and to make sure that you share your beliefs and feelings with each other. Otherwise, both the sex and money issues can become major conflicts which can destroy even the deepest love.

8. TRY TO GET ALONG WITH EACH OTHER'S FRIENDS AND FAMILIES

Although your happiness ultimately depends on how well the two of you get along with each other, some input from loved ones can be the frosting on the cake. Do you have a healthy interaction with each other's close associates? Make sure you ask some supportive family members and/or dear friends of their opinion about your choice in pursuing their loved one. If the advice is not what you want to hear, examine it closely, evaluate the source, think about it, and make up your own mind anyway. Make sure you also meet your partner's family and closest friends, and discreetly observe their interactions with each other. Look to see if there is any dysfunctional family pattern that you need to address or get help with. There is an old saying, "Show me your company, I'll tell you who you are." Chances are, if your partner has a healthy interaction with loved ones, you will also get the same treatment--and much more!

9. STAY AWAY FROM NEGATIVE PEOPLE

It's important to make a special note here, that although the interactions of relatives and friends can be a plus in building a healthy relationship, some, unfortunately, can also be a minus. If you face unhealthy interference and discouragement from loved ones because of their personal insecurities, don't let them have any influence in your relationship. Both you and your partner must be on the same page and decide to keep negative people out of your personal love life in order to love and grow together in a harmonious, healthy relationship.

10. LEARN TO LAUGH TOGETHER

This one doesn't need much explanation; if there's no joy, there's very little hope. Laughter keeps love alive. Find something that you can both get a good hearty laugh from. Here's a little secret that works wonders: A good sense of humor and a pleasant disposition has a magnetic attraction that makes people always want to be in your presence. How can that special person resist your gorgeous smile and sparkling eyes? Go ahead, laugh a bit--have fun and enjoy.

A healthy relationship is one where the two of you can be yourselves and have nothing to hide about. A healthy relationship is one where there is general support. It is not about every man or woman for themself. In healthy relationships, couples support each other in all ways. Be it financially, physically, emotionally and any kind of support that is needed. No one in the relationship should be afraid to ask for help just because they think they will look weak and the partner might end up looking down upon them. Everyone needs help once in a while, even the strongest ones sometimes need help. A healthy relationship is one where a partner is not afraid to ask for it and will not feel guilty about asking for it; nor will they feel like they are disturbing their partner. That is as long as it is something you really need help with.

A healthy relationship is rare these days. Many of us have forgotten what it means to have one. Reminding ourselves of these healthy relationship tips will make our current relationships better than ever.

CHAPTER 8

CHIVALRY IS NOT DEAD YET, APPRECIATE THE LITTLE THINGS

Chivalry is not dead. It is still quivering with anticipation somewhere, waiting to be engaged in service. However, it is being suppressed by each of the following:

1. Equality of the sexes: May younger women no longer wish to have anything done on their behalf, no matter how simple. There is the misguided notion that every male who might wish to do something for a woman, because he admires her or just wishes to be courteous, has an ulterior motive. Women feel increasingly compromised or obliged by such actions and so there are fewer opportunities to be chivalrous. Don't let this be you. Appreciate the ones who open doors for you or offer small favors. It doesn't mean they're automatically looking for sex, it's very possible they're just being nice, as it's how they were raised.

2. Distrust and Suspicion: Everyone comes under the spotlight as being guilty before being innocent these days.

We no longer accept behavior at face value, especially when it comes from the opposite sex. We tend to question attitude, motives, and actions much more than we used to do which then demotivates men to do anything at all for fear of being negatively labeled or rejected. Just take a breath, relax, and look at the situation from an analytical, logical, and non fallacious point of view. Keep emotion out of it and judge something by fact, not opinion.

3. Lack of personal confidence and self esteem: People who are low in esteem may be unsure as to how to handle chivalrous acts. They feel embarrassed by compliments; they tend to focus on themselves and are also not sure how to react in the face of any chivalry. Many people lack self-love and so, when they are treated in very caring ways, they are apt to doubt the sincerity of the giver. Not used to giving to themselves, and more likely to be self-conscious, low confidence people are likely to ignore chivalrous acts or to interpret them as suspicious.

4. The age we live in: There is far less emphasis on 'gentlemanly' qualities these days. Young boys are brought up just to be themselves, no longer as 'gentlemen', a state which is now more familiar to older men and to which they used to aspire. The social protocol of behaving like a gentleman and being there for a lady has been lost in many parts of the world. With it goes the kind of actions that demarcated gentlemen and made them much sought after. The days of standing up when a

woman enters the room, holding doors, and pushing in chairs have been on the decline for years.

Chivalry is still there smoldering in many corners, but, as with everything in society, we have to accept that the interpretation of what it means to be chivalrous can also change and be dictated by the expectations of the age we are in.

CHAPTER 9

WHY DO MEN CHEAT?

A ccording to statistics, reports show that men cheat more than a woman (or are just caught more often). This may or may not be surprising to you. The question here is why. This is not something that has been definitely nailed down, but there is one reason that seems to stand out from the rest. Read on to find out the most common reason that men cheat in relationships.

THE REASON

Most women tend to feel it is their fault that their man is cheating. This leads to the woman feeling bad about herself and causes problems with self-esteem. The truth is that the top reason men cheat have nothing to do with the woman they are with. The most common reason that men cheat is that men have a natural drive to seek out various sexual partners. They may seek out someone who has a quality their current partner lacks, but draws them in.

Men seem to be biologically inclined to cheat. It is controllable, though, since there are many men that do not cheat. However, for some men, this biological draw is too strong for them to handle. They may not even mean to hurt the woman they are with, but that is always what seems to happen. Does this mean they should get a free pass? Absolutely not.

HOW TO SPOT CHEATING

Spotting cheating is not always easy. It can be made difficult if the man has cheated before. However, there is some truth to the old saying once a cheater, always a cheater, because once a man gives into the natural tendency, they may have a hard time deflecting it in the future. Usually, you will have a feeling or see changes in your partner that signal he is cheating. You may even see obvious signs such as lipstick stains on clothing or the smell of strange perfume. You may even get calls from his mistress. Sometimes a mistress will actually talk to you and tell you what is going on and other times they can simply hang up.

HOW TO DEAL WITH CHEATING?

When you suspect that your man is cheating, you need to deal with it. Now, I'm not saying you need to bring him onto some lousy talk show or have a radio host confront him about your suspicions.. You have to gather proof or facts and bring them up in a respectful matter. Also, you need to make sure that you are prepared to handle what comes after you get him to admit he has cheated.

Before you confront him, you need to realize that he may try to explain away all his actions and the proof you have. Either this, or he may flat out tell you the truth. Please keep in mind that just because you suspect something, doesn't mean it's actually happening. Hear him out and form your own LOGICAL (not emotional) conclusions. You have to be ready to either counter these and get to the truth, or accept them at face value. I know these ideas are not easy to implement, but they are doable. It will take commitment on your part to get to know these materials..

CHAPTER 10

PHYSICAL AND EMOTIONAL ATTRACTIVENESS

Physical attraction is important. Not only in the sense that men are visual learners and it helps to look good to get their attention, but because it will boost your self confidence as well. However, just looking pretty alone will not keep his interest for very long.

The attraction goes a whole lot deeper than just looking good. I am sure that you have noticed that there are many gorgeous women who always seem to be having relationship problems, so clearly looking good isn't the only thing to do with having a lasting, healthy, happy relationship. The attraction a man has for you is nothing that he can control either. In other words, he will either feel it for you or he won't. Unfortunately, there is no middle ground with this one.

Because it is nothing that he can control, women can use that knowledge to their advantage!

So what kind of attraction do you need to build with the man in your life and how do you do that? You need to build massive emotional attraction with him. This is how you inspire a man to be interested in being with you and only you. The emotional attraction you build with him has to do with how you make him feel when he is around you.

In essence, you have to make him feel good when around you so that he has fun when he is with you and remembers the good times you spent together when he is away from you. That way when he is away from you, he keeps thinking about you and every time he thinks of you, he cannot help but smile and wonder when the next time is that he will be able to talk to you or see you.

It's easy to build this attraction if you remember that if he feels good being with you, he will stay. If he feels bad being with you, he will go (and sometimes faster than you can blink).

SO HOW DO YOU BUILD EMOTIONAL ATTRACTION WITH A MAN?

1. Play with him: Make sure that you have lots of fun together. Always keep him smiling. When he is smiling, everything is good. This tip may sound incredibly simplistic, but it is really very powerful.

2. Give him as much space as you can. Enjoy the time you have when you are together. Have fun and live in the moment, but do not crowd him. Pull back sometimes and allow him to miss you, to wonder about you and to come looking for you. Let him have fun with that sometimes. Enjoy the magic when he finds you.

3. Be interesting and unpredictable. Be provocative, sometimes with what you say and do so that he never quite knows what you will say or do next. That way he cannot help but think about you because you keep him guessing.

4. Take things slow. It doesn't matter how much fun you are having with him; do not try to rush ahead by forcing your feelings on him. The key here is staying one step behind him and two steps ahead. This is how you keep him on his toes.

Building emotional attraction is as much fun for you as it is for him and in the end, you both get what you want.

HOW CAN YOU STOP NAGGING; TIPS FOR MEN, AND WOMEN?

Nagging: "To be a persistent source of annoyance or distraction. To irritate by constant scolding or urging." That is the definition from Merriam-Webster.

This is what an individual feels when they think they are being "nagged". Who wants to deal with the constant annoyance and scolding? Not any grown adult I know. So what is the root of nagging? Depending on where you look, you may find different answers, but from what I've learned, nagging is a result of a lack of communication between two partners.

It is a way for one person to actually elicit a response from the other, albeit a negative response. When one partner feels like communication is failing, and they need some sort of interaction from their other half, they resort to any means necessary to get some interaction.

Nagging is one way to achieve this. They ride you and pester you until finally, you retaliate with anger and frustration. It worked for them; they got you to say something. They now know you are listening to them, and that's really all they wanted. They wanted some attention, to know you hear them. What they hope for is a positive exchange between the two of you, and feel that negative communication is better than no communication.

Everyone has a need to feel wanted, needed, and important to someone else. That is a big reason why we choose to be with our spouse in the first place. We love that they care for us, want to be with us, understand us, and want to grow with us. When those feelings subside, we begin to feel very insecure. We miss the interaction, compassion, conversation and love that we grew so accustomed to. We crave that energy, and we want it back. Instead of expressing that we need attention, we can fall into the nagging phase. Afraid to rock the boat more permanently, we feel nagging is more short term. So we nag until we get the same response (attention) from our spouse. And this leads to a fight or argument and snowballs the feelings of insecurity on both parties.

Can nagging, then, lead to an affair? The answer is absolute yes! And the affair could come from either spouse. This is because when nagging occurs, it is a sign that the basic needs of husband and wife (or boyfriend and girlfriend) are not being met. You are not giving your spouse the attention they need, the feeling of security, and so on and so forth.

Likewise, they feel that you are not providing them with those same needs, and thus they nag you until you come through for them. When basic needs aren't being met, physically or emotionally, a spouse will seek alternative means to satisfy those needs. This is how affairs happen. If you fail to pay attention to your spouse, show sincere interest in them, and let them know how important you are to them, they will find someone who can provide these essential needs. This may come in the form of emotional cheating or physical cheating.

How can you overcome this? I suggest you each sit down (individually) and write down what "your" marriage profile is. A marriage profile is simply what you expect your marriage to be like. Start out from the time you wake up until the time you go to bed. Describe how your ideal day would go and where and how your spouse is included in that day. If your spouse isn't included, then that's another problem in itself.

Ask yourself these questions along the way:

Do you share a meaningful conversation with your spouse when you wake up or do you just get ready for work?

Do you eat meals together? Home or Out?

Do you call your spouse throughout the day or just wait until you get home?

Do you think about your spouse during the day?

Do you plan what you and your spouse will do later during the day or week? Any dates with your spouse?

What do your conversations consist of?

How many minutes during the day are you sharing meaningful conversation with your spouse?

What activities do you do with your spouse?

How do you end your evening with your spouse?

Do you have a meaningful conversation before bed?

How happy are you after this "ideal" day?

Writing these things out and creating a profile is essential to happiness. Now, see what your spouse has written and compare. This type of activity will create meaningful conversation and ideally bring back the spark you are missing. Constant nagging is a sign that something is wrong in your relationship, and you need to address it before one partner decides to either have an affair or end it. You just learned a great exercise to help build a better, more trusting relationship with your partner. Practice this exercise and you can help eliminate nagging in your relationship.

CONCLUSION

Does your man seem disinterested when you are trying to talk to him about something vital to you? Do you feel that you too have a problem and you wish to discuss it? Does your man seem less than excited when you insist you both must talk about the issue right then and there?

Men, more often than not, wish to keep their problems to themselves and think about them for a while. It does not mean your man is incapable of communicating with you, it just means that he would rather process the situation before saying anything. More often than not, a man will need to come up with something concrete to say or a specific solution to a problem, rather than just discussing several different options with you. Though women often think about their problems out loud and wish to discuss or talk about every aspect of an issue, it does not mean men have to do the same. When it comes to communicating, give your man some space. When he is ready to talk to you about an issue, permit him to approach you. Remind yourself that you are two different creatures and when it comes down to it, men and women have a very different style of communication. Sometimes, talking about an issue isn't always the best way to resolve it. Sometimes, the best response to a problem is time.

Do not be offended when you don't get exactly the response you would expect or desire. Guys are not easy to figure out at first. The next time you are upset with your man, try to think about it the way he would. Simply acknowledging that men think in different ways can lift off a heavy burden from your shoulders. The next time he reacts differently to what you would expect, don't sweat the small stuff. It doesn't mean that he doesn't care. He just thinks differently than the way you do.

Understanding men really isn't all that complicated when you break it down this way. It truly is a matter of widening your horizons and accepting another person's point of view. Once you can accept that, you'll be well on your way to having a relationship that has a true chance of succeeding.

SOME FINAL THOUGHTS

Bad Boys

Just stop chasing the bad boys. Yes, almost every girl goes through a bad boy phase where they love the thrill of dating that one guy who gets in trouble or hangs out with the tough crowd. It's not worth it, nor does it make you look cool. Don't justify it by convincing yourself that you can change him. Maybe you can, but in the end it may just be a wasted few years of life before you realize you left a lot of decent guys on the sidelines, while trying to straighten out that mess you started dating in high school. Just get it out of your system early and move on.

He Looked at Another Girl!

Ladies.. Just because your man looks or glances at another woman passing by, does not mean he's being unfaithful or wants to run over and pounce on her. It is in no way meant to be a sign of disrespect to you or an insult in any way when he does this. Everyone can appreciate a good looking individual, and let's face it, there are better looking people in the world than the one you're dating. It's okay for women to look at guys, and for guys to look at women. As the old saying goes "It's okay to look at the menu, as long as you eat at home".

Spell it out for Him

In reality, some guys just don't get it. They may never understand you, and in turn, it makes it that much more difficult for you to understand them. To some guys, you might as well be the equivalent of solving a Rubik's cube behind your back with your hands cuffed in front of you while a foreigner is yelling at you in another language. To many guys, this is how it is. Help him out; spell it out for him. Tell him what you like and don't like. Tell them what your expectations are and don't keep him guessing if it's clearly not working.

The First Move

I get it, traditionally speaking, the guy is supposed to make the first move. Now, this may come as a surprise to some but NOT

ALL GUYS ARE CONFIDENT (yes, that was sarcastic). If you're interested, just help the poor guy out and kiss him already. This may just be what he needed to spark his confidence. Don't wait days or weeks for him to do something he clearly wants to do but is too afraid for fear of getting slapped or rejected because he's too naïve to read the obvious signs in front of him. Don't beat around the bush; be blunt with what you want. Sometimes, you'll know it before he does. This goes for both sides of the relationship.

With that being said, have fun in a relationship. If it stops being fun, find out why and try to fix it. It's a two way street and it works both ways. If it's still not working, move on. There are plenty of fish in the sea and believe it or not, there are loads of people out there that you would be completely and utterly happy to fall in love and spend the rest of your life with.

HOW TO UNDERSTAND WOMEN

The Secret Behind How They Think
And What They Really Want

BY K. CONNORS

TABLE OF CONTENT

INTRODUCTION

Before we begin, please feel free to check out some of my other work such as How to Understand Men if you're interested in learning more about men as well!

Do you have a hard time understanding women? Why are women so complicated? Why do nice guys always seem to finish last? Why do women like some guys better than others? Trying to get a girl to like you, or not understanding why a particular girl doesn't like you back can really suck. If you're asking yourself the question "Why won't she date me?" or "What does he have that I don't?".. You're not alone. Or, maybe you've already secured the relationship and really just want to know what she means when she says one thing, but then gets upset when you do it or agree.

The only thing you really can be sure of is: Women are COMPLICATED. You meet a woman who seems to like you and tells you you're a great guy. You see her regularly and start hanging out with her. You really like her so you get up the nerve to ask her out on an actual date, and she turns you down. Why? What did you do wrong? Or what could you have done differently? Why do the women who seem to genuinely like you never want to date you? Why do you keep ending up in the Friend Zone? Attraction isn't a choice, and you know that's true. If a girl you liked well enough (but wasn't your "type") were to ask you for a date, you would be flattered. However, would it make you say yes?

WHAT'S GOING ON?

Just because a girl compliments you and tells you you're a nice guy, doesn't mean she's into you. It's an honest, but tough fact of life that girls don't find men sexually attractive nearly as often as guys do girls. I know that for guys, it sucks, but it's just the way it is. In fact, when a girl tells you you're a nice guy, warning bells should be ringing. It might be her way of telling you she likes you, but it's more likely her way of saying that she's never going to get hot and bothered about you. The way girls communicate is very different from that of men. Girls are nurturers and carers, and they recoil from saying unpleasant things straight out (most of the time).

Instead, they will try to soften the blow by saying something nice and leave you to work out that the real truth that lies in what they're not saying. The thing is that girls hint at unpleasant truths far more often that telling them outright.

Any other girl will have no trouble picking up on the hint and understand the real meaning of what was said. Unfortunately, girls expect men to be able to do the same. Of course, they can't - and don't.

So when a girl says 'You're a really nice guy' she's trying to let you down gently, because the unspoken ending to that sentence has been often 'So I don't really know why I don't fancy you - but I just don't'. And in case you're wondering, she really does mean the bit about thinking you're a nice guy, and hopes it will make you feel a bit better.

HOW TO UNDERSTAND WOMEN

Becoming a girl's friend isn't the way to her heart, although many men hope that it might be. When you play the part of friend and confidante, you are diminishing your masculinity in her eyes, even if neither of you know it. To attract a woman sexually you need to make her aware of your masculinity; to remind her that she is a member of the opposite sex. This goes back to the very basics of human interation and evolution, where a female is attracted to the dominant male. It's this consciousness that creates sexual attraction. Make it clear that you are looking for a girlfriend, not another buddy. At the very least, it will remind her of what you are, and it may make her look at you in a new light. Flirt with her, tease her and make her laugh, but don't cozy up to her and try to be her friend. Girls don't fall in love with their friends (Okay, maybe in Hollywood, but this is real life). They fall in love with men. What else do women look for in men? Find out more about what women really want, so that you can strike some real sparks with the next girl you pursue.

Let's get started.

CHAPTER ONE

HOW TO UNDERSTAND WOMEN

When it comes to how to understand women, the first thought that comes to mind is that women are the complex sex. However, it is difficult to imagine life without women, and no matter how hard it may be, one cannot but help try to understand them. There are so many variables that it may be difficult to internalize all of them. The reality is that most men make the mistake of assuming things on the basis of what they see. A woman's appearance may be completely contradictory to what she has on the inside. Women like to dress the way they want and in the way they believe brings out the best in them. For example, a woman may choose to look feminine on the outside, but will have a completely different personality on the inside, or vice-versa.

The best advice on how to understand women is to remember that no two women are alike. They are individuals, just like men. The phrase "you're just like every other guy" doesn't hold much weight when it comes to fmales. Men understanding women is just as difficult as it is the other way round. Women find it difficult to understand men too. If you want to understand women, listen to them. Now, listening does not mean that you keep watching television while she is pouring her heart out and telling you all about how she feels. To understand her feelings, you need to listen attentively. Ask questions when need be and apply your mind. This is of particular importance because there is a vast difference between how women and men feel and how they interpret situations.

Another thing that can help you understand women is to spend time with them. Make friends with women at work, try to meet as many as you can, or socialize with them. Try different things to attract women and get them in your life. The more time you spend with them, the easier it will be to understand them. It goes without saying that to do that, you need to be comfortable in the presence of a woman and overcome that irrational fear of that many of you have.

Ask questions. Believe it or not, most women appreciate the fact that you are taking the time to learn more about them, showing a genuine interest in what they have to say. Let her know that you know little about women, and let your curiosity be your guide to understanding them. After that, you are on your own and it depends on you as to how you analyze the information you gather first hand.

Women do cry more and are more expressive. It's a fact. At the same time, women are more skilled than men when it comes to understanding the needs of other people, including their children.

Despite all this, it is still doubtful whether we will ever understand women fully. What is more important is to understand the woman who matters most to you, i.e. the one with whom you want to spend a lifetime with.

THE SIMPLEST WAY TO UNDERSTAND WOMEN

There are a lot of different ways for you to learn about women. Understanding them, however, is something that takes some people a lifetime. If you're going to pursue this knowledge, and you truly want to know how to deal with them and understand how to navigate the different elements that make them who they are, take the following tips to heart. It all starts with focusing on what you want out of your understanding.

1. PAY CLOSE ATTENTION TO THEIR ACTIONS

The first thing that you should do is simple; look at what they do. Consider where they go, what they do, and what is habitual for them. People assume that it's very difficult to learn how to understand women, but it all starts with paying attention to what they are doing. The more you know about their actions, the higher the chances are that you will understand why they do things, which will lead to larger understanding women in general.

2. ASK THEM QUESTIONS

If you're serious about pursuing a particular individual, then you need to ask them pointed questions. Ask them why, in reference to what they are doing, and how they feel in certain situations.

You'll find that the simplest way to learn is to just ask. Asking questions should be simple, done with confidence, and with a focus on understanding.

3. DON'T GET TOO SURPRISED WITH THE CHANGES

Just because you have asked, paid attention, and think you know.. you don't. One thing about women is that they change their minds a great deal, and one day they may shock you with a change. Your goal is to not be shocked. Don't make reference to changing things up. Instead, just pay attention to how the change occurs, and what it means overall. As you look into it, you'll end up with a positive overall learning experience. At the end of the day, you're going to need to take your time with the process of learning how to understand women. In order to do this, you'll need to pay attention to what you're told, the actions that women take, and how they react to certain things that you do. The biggest step here is to simply pay attention.

4. FIND OUT WHAT SHE WANTS AND GIVE IT TO HER

Women do want a gentleman, so give her one. The secret is not to overdo it. Being thoughtful and there for her is great, but you have to instill limits. Don't kill yourself trying to be at her every beck and call; you must give her breathing room and time to herself. If you are "always there" for her you can begin to emasculate yourself and become as much a (girl) friend as anything else. She may be great, but I assume you would rather date her than take her to get her nails done on the weekends.

5. UNDERSTAND WOMEN - THERE ARE WAYS THEY ARE LIKE MEN

Don't make yourself so easy. I'm sure you have seen it; there is always "that girl", that you don't personally find attractive, someone you do not desire, that you know you could get if you put some effort into it. Why don't you pursue her? It is not about the looks as much as you might think. It is about the challenge. No one wants something that is easy. A 1/2 mile walk through the park is no accomplishment.

A 1/2 mile of the arduous free climb up the side of a mountain is the stuff legends are made of. Keep obstacles up. Do not make it seem like your affection is an easy thing to get. Get her to respect you, not pity you.

6. DO NOT CLING. SHE NEEDS TIME APART.

Clinging around too often is too much! She may even think (and say) that she wants you around 24/7. But if you are around too much it is very easy to get bored. Familiarity breeds contempt, as they say. Keep a certain distance from her until you have been dating a long time. Then, spend a ton of time and see if you can break it. You'll see what the difference is once you experience it for yourself.

7. UNDERSTAND WOMEN THROUGH BODY LANGUAGE

When a man is interested or in love with a womawn, he will eventually do anything just to find out the interests and hobbies of said woman. Men want to know if the women they want to be with are interested in them or not. In order to know the art of understanding a woman's mind and body, you should learn how women show their gestures, especially in terms of body language or non-verbal communication. This is very important if you want a woman you like to stay with you. There are many ways to determine a woman's body language to know if she into you or just another friend.

The most common gesture that women use is eye contact. If she looks at you for more than a few seconds unbroken, then you may have something there. If you are talking to her, and she stares at you deeply, then it shows that she is interested in earing what you have to say. There are times that she will blink her eyes when you are talking. However, if she is looking at somebody else or doing other things while you are talking, she may not be interested in you. Let's say you're on a date or having a meal with a particular lady. If she purposely pokes your feet or gently touches you while you are talking, odds are she may be into you. Or she's just clumsy.. Crossed legs can be read a few different ways. One, it could mean she is shy or not comfortable yet with the situation. It my also be a formality during a nice evening or dinner. I prefer not to read into this one too much, as it can give mixed signals. If she walks away or increases her distance to you while you were sitting then it clearly means that she doesn't like you. There are also times that she will mimic some of your actions like facial gestures or hand movements. This coupled with eye contact is a good sign.

Moreover, if you two are talking while walking, and she moves away from you or moves behind, then it clearly means that she doesn't enjoy being with you.

If she stays beside you then it could mean that she likes you. Women have many gestures to express their feelings for a guy, although women do vary from methods and principles of showing their affection. In short, a basic knowledge of psychology is needed to know if they are into you or not.

8. WOMEN DON'T ALWAYS MEAN WHAT THEY SAY AND SAY WHAT THEY MEAN

Now, this is a tricky one and most guy pay too much attention to what women actually say. You see, this is where most guys make a huge mistake. Women aren't always honest about what they want in a guy; in fact, a great deal of the time they don't even know what they want. Ever been in a situation where a woman told you that she wants to be with a nice caring guy, but is actually in the company of a complete jerk? Does this make sense at all? NO! However, you see this all too common scenario in our present day society.

Therefore, if you really want to know what women truly want in a guy or want to figure them out, just focus on her actions. If a woman says that she wants a nice guy, yet she always falls for the bad kind, then don't waste your time.

Bottom line: The truth is in what she does...Not always what she says.

Therefore, the more you focus on her actions the easier it will be to figure her out. For example, if she says that she doesn't really like you, but always calls you consistently and goes out with you regardless, then it's obvious that she has something going on for you, even if she doesn't say it. However, it is still important to keep in mind that looming dark cloud called "The Friend Zone". More on this later..

Now listen carefully; what you are about to discover in this book, most men will never know when it comes to attracting women. This is one thing which is an absolute must know for every man out there. I don't care if you're bald, fat, ugly, blue, small, or have 3 eyes.. You are about to discover an ultimate secret weapon which will make women chase you around like crazy!

CHAPTER TWO

WHAT WOMEN REALLY WANT FROM A MAN

No one ever really is 100% sure about what they want. Sometimes it is a spur of the moment decision. Sometimes it takes half of your lifetime to make that decision. But either way, we never really are sure about what we want. Women are particularly indecisive. Because they are highly unpredictable about what they want, you should tread very carefully. Don't always assume that you know what they want just from careful observations - sometimes those aren't enough.

A spur of the moment decision is what a woman wants in a man. Sometimes it's during those nights when she sees him across the dance floor, all flared up and ready to go. She'll probably say, "That's how I want my man to be - always cool and spontaneous." Or those sudden random acts of kindness will get a "Oh, how sweet. That's what I want in a man." Because of a traumatic past experience in relationships, some women become hesitant with what they want. She might even become fearful because of what happened in the past and may not be in any state fit for a new relationship.

Putting all these aside again, no one ever really knows what they want. If her tastes for a man have changed, it sometimes means she has become refined, going for the steady jobs and the retirement planner. Sometimes, when she becomes indecisive, it's like she's speed shopping and just simply wants to grab anything and everything off the shelf, not even bothering to see if it's the right one or not.

You can never be one or the other or all for someone. They have to chose you because they found something in you that they couldn't find in anyone else.

Some women love fairy tales and romance movies, or books because they are hopeless romantics. They love stories of men defying the odds to win the woman of their dreams. They dream of their prince charming in shining armor to fall down to their knees and woo them.

You should know what she wants to be able to connect with her. Knowing what she really wants from her man makes it easier to win her heart.

The following tips can be very helpful to know what women really want from their men.

5. ATTENTION: Attention is what she really wants. Most women want their men to focus on them. She may not say it or demand it from you in an obvious manner, but women love to have your thoughts, your time, and your complete and undivided attention. It is true that life is not all about

love, and there are many things that can distract men such as work, friends, and hobbies. Despite all these things, you have to make her feel like she is more important than anything else in the world and that you think about her even if she's not with you. You also have to give her your 100% undivided attention if she is with you. Send her flowers or food to her work or stop by her office and take her out for her lunch break once in a while. It is not the things that you gave her that makes her feel special, but the efforts and the attention you've been giving her.

6. THOUGHTFULNESS: What she really wants from her man is thoughtfulness. You should remember even the smallest of details about her that most people don't care about. Knowing the type of movies she likes, books she usually reads, her shoe size, her favorite flowers, her family members' birthdays or parents' anniversaries, her daily coffee order, how she likes her eggs done, etc. Remembering small details about a woman makes her feel loved. It is a sign that you really care and are interested in what makes her happy. Every woman's heart melts for a man like this.

7. ADMIRATION: What she really wants from her man is his admiration. Many women are not confident with their looks and their personalities so they want to be admired and desired. Make her feel like she is the most beautiful woman for you. Don't just say it, believe it! Of course, you have to be sincere about it and not just for the sake of making her feel good. Compliment her with her best physical features like

her hair, her skin and everything you find attractive about her.

8. LOVE: What she really wants from her man is his love. Women need to feel and hear that they are well-loved. Many men aren't good at expressing their feelings of love and they are not vocal about it, but women want their men to be expressive and vocal about their affection towards them. Love can be expressed in so many ways, but she also needs to hear the words "I love you" from you so you need to be vocal with your feelings. She needs to be reminded that you are still in love with her. If you don't do or say these things, she will get worried that you don't mean it or that she's doing something wrong. Don't force her to overthink!

9. SECURITY: Security, security, security! Women crave this from a man and this is your key to success. What she wants is to know that you will always be there no matter what! You have to prove it not just with words, but also by actions. She wants to know that you will be there for her even if she screams at you, becomes unreasonable, or does not make sense! Well, to you anyway.. She wants you to be a man because that will help her feel like a woman. When she was growing up, she had a vision of the perfect man, one that would sweep her off her feet and look after her forever. This is a secure feeling and she craves it. When you help her feel like a woman she will stop at nothing to make you feel like a man, this is fantastic for your relationship and is what you are both after.

Relationships need to be nurtured to last and it is important that you know how to make your partner feel loved and to keep the fire burning in your relationship. Keep the romance alive!

CHAPTER THREE

WHY CONFIDENCE MATTERS

Confidence matters. It matters because when someone has natural confidence people around them feel confident about them in return. For example, if you were approached by a person confident in themselves and their relationship, it is easy to start trusting what they are saying. Imagine the difference between speaking to someone who is confident and someone who mumbles something while shuffling their feet and looking at the floor. It is hard to think anything but "they are not very sure about their business, and if they aren't why should I be?" Working with your strengths, really understanding all the fabulous things about you, and then building on these is great ways to bring positivity into your life.

To me, there are six areas which affect confidence in life, relationships, and in business.

1. DISSATISFACTION

Even when life seems terrible, there are always great things happening, and it pays to focus on these as opposed to the bad.

Asking for what you really want means you'll probably start working towards getting it, creating satisfaction.

2. REJECTION

Consider that what someone else thinks, does, and says is a reflection of their perceptions, life experiences, values, and beliefs. This is more about them and less about you. It helps.

3. PERFECTION

Is perfection really going to make that much difference? Having far more confidence will enable you to do your absolute best. Do this with what you have and don't worry about what you don't. Have a go; it really does make a difference.

4. WORRY

Worry and fear are feelings you don't want. It is often far more productive to focus on what you do want, put an action plan in place, and just do it. When worry and fear come around, take a step back and ask yourself why. Keep in mind, you miss 100% of the shots you don't take.

5. VICTIM MENTALITY

Taking ownership of yourself, your decisions, your thoughts, and your life creates a sense of empowerment. Empowerment promotes confidence and puts you in the driving seat. Don't play the victim card. No one likes it and it doesn't get you anywhere.

6. HELPLESSNESS

Being in control of yourself and your life direction is a great confidence booster. Start by forgetting the outcomes you cannot possibly influence and work on the ones you can.

CHAPTER FOUR

WHY NICE GUYS LOSE MORE THAN THEY SHOULD

There are many men that feel they are a nice guy and that women are crazy to pass them over. You see, the problem is that nice guys put themselves on some sort of pedestal. Nice guys like to think they are superior to other men or that they are better in relationships, and that by virtue of their niceness are more deserving of a woman's romantic attentions. This may be true in some cases, or even most cases, but that superior mindset isn't going to get you where you want to go.

Most of the time, nice guys are not as nice as they like to think. Some nice guys are whiny, close-minded, judgmental, spineless, controlling, and weak. Women do not like weak, whiny, judgmental men. Ergo, women do not like nice guys.

Women want men; decisive, action-oriented, determined, and aggressive. Sadly, sometimes that comes bundled with a liar and a cheater which is what the nice guys point to as the reason they say women are crazy. But who said that every woman should want a nice guy? Who made that a law? Why do nice guys condemn women for choosing thrill seeking, impulsive men with a bad boy edge? In other words, the choices that exclude nice guys.

Being a nice guy does not win you any brownie points in the dating game! Maybe right off the bat, but it isn't sustainable. Unless, a nice guy is what she wants. You win at dating when you give the opposite sex what they want. Even if a woman is your wife, you still have to have a spine and stand strong, while remaining in control of yourself as you should. The bottom line that you nice guys need to understand is this: when women are young they are not interested in settling down and being serious. Why would a girl want some clingy, overly solicitous codependent around? Young women want to have fun. And the best men to have fun with are impulsive thrill seekers that have an edge; males that exude testosterone and inspire passion and desire with their games and lies. Which is why nice guys that project neediness, that go out of their way to please women with the expectation of getting something in return get passed over.

I was so nice to her, why doesn't she love me? I deserve to have someone love me more than those players do!" the nice guys say.

No, you don't. But, if you want to get the girls you need to give her whatever it is that she wants. I'm not saying some women don't want a nice guy; I'm saying that the majority, whether they know ir or not, or disagree, don't want a nice guy. Certainly, in a marital partnership, there is established trust and decisions are made with the input from both parties for the betterment of the family. But we are talking about dating here, not marriage.

When a woman loses respect for a man, she loses her sexual attraction for him as well. She sees you as a brother or a friend. You are subsequently put in The Friend Zone and you are never coming out. If the two were dating, she will ultimately declare that "he's too nice" and dump him out of boredom.

There is hope for you guys though. Bad boy types stay exciting for a few years, and then most women move on. Once the play is out of their system (just like in guys), people change their perspectives on life. Their choices in lifestyle, dress, and romantic partners change as well. As a woman heads into her late 20s and 30s, she transitions and begins to look for a husband and father for her children. She will look for slightly different qualities in her mate and put more emphasis and higher value on personal qualities like honesty, work ethic, family values, responsibility, and similar lifestyle than she does on excitement and sex appeal. However, even if a woman is middle-aged, she does not want a weak, whiny, judgmental guy! Every woman on this planet wants a guy that she sees as attractive, exciting and sexy; she just wants him to be committed and devoted to her and the kids at the same time (assuming children are involved).

Finding the right woman for you is simply a matter of you matching whatever it is that a woman is looking for. If you fit her needs, you're in. No matter how "nice" a guy you might perceive yourself to be, you still may not be the right guy for her.

NOW LET'S WORK ON FIXING IT.

Are you a nice guy? The kind of guy that every woman should want to bring home to mom and dad? Do your friends tell you that you deserve better when you get rejected and do have lots of friends who are women, but who simply "don't like you like that"? If this is you, guess what?

You are suffering from a severe case of being too "bland to bring to bed". Let's work on fixing it, and start doing it right now. Look, I'm just going to be honest, ok? I don't want hurt anyone's feelings, but sometimes tough love is in order. Being nice is great. Being a pushover though, is not. Often "nice" is simply a euphemism for boring. Remember when they used to say a woman had a "great personality" before you met her? Well, that's what they are saying about you, and we all know it's the kiss of death for getting a hot, in demand woman who has her choice of options. She is almost always going to jump to a nice guy who also happens to have an edge, is exciting and lives a little dangerously, too.

Here are some things you can do right now.. Start taking some chances in life. Go out on the edge a little bit. Be more adventurous and learn a little bit. Take risks. Remember the dare-devil careless attitude you had as a kid? Get it back. The dare-devil is very sexy if he's got a sweet side too.. Hey, I'm not going to tell you to go out and get a few tattoos and a Harley to go with that electrical engineering degree, but a free spirit attitude and a willingness to have fun will get you much further than a box of candy and some flowers. Combine the both and you've got the perfect recipe.

Look, you are a good guy. And that is something most girls want. But, they need an edge to stay interested. I can't tell you how many quality guys I know eventually "settle" for far less than someone they could have gotten with a little bit of spice mixed into their game. And you can learn this stuff, too...even if it's not your natural personality. You can fake it till you make it and she'll be totally head over heels in love with you before she realizes you're simply a sweetheart after all. Nice guys can finish first, after all, if they know how to be bad once in a while.

CHAPTER FIVE

WHY DO WOMEN LIKE BAD BOYS?

Have you ever noticed that bad boys seem to date more women than nice guys? Ever wondered why women seem to be more attracted to men who treat them badly than to those who treat them nicely? Well, no one ever said women made sense, but the whole phenomenon is actually very simple. There's a reason why it's not a very good idea to be "too nice" to a woman. The more you try to be nice to her, the more she'll see you as a friend and nothing more. Why? Simply because you're making her feel the same way she feels whenever she's around her friends.

Of course, this doesn't mean that you have to be the opposite of nice and start treating her badly; far from it. You might end up losing her much more quickly this way.

Dating bad boys is quite unpredictable. He may take her out to a restaurant one minute and the next minute have a risky ride on his motorcycle. Some women find a safe and comfortable ride quite boring. Women feel quite sexy while dating bad boys. The main reason behind this is that bad boys do not care whether a woman likes them or not. Now compare this to a so-called nice guy who is always desperate to please his lady and can come across as clingy and wimpy. Breaking rules is common among bad boys and this automatically makes them attractive to women who are thrilled with the unpredictable and exciting behavior. Whereas good guys are predictable and this can get boring.

Women who love bad boys actually get subconsciously attracted to their self-confidence. In this way, the gene factor also plays an important role in attraction to bad boys. One thing is certain; being bad gets more attraction at a young age than being good.

WHY DO GIRLS LIKE BAD BOYS?

If you ask most females why they like bad boys they'll say the challenge, the excitement or the thrill of living vicariously. Some will think that they can "change" him and make him better. Often what starts out as an exciting high-speed adventure ends up turning into an emotionally draining dramatic relationshit. Bad boys offer a double dosage of pain and pleasure. When they're bad they're downright awful, but when they are good they make you feel like you've just hit the lotto. Here are the most common reasons that women like bad boys.

1. SECRET FEAR OF INTIMACY

If a girl is attracted to guys who they cannot really have because they don't want a real relationship or they're involved with someone else - perhaps they have a secret fear of intimacy. The reason they may find a bad boy so appealing is because they can be with him without ever letting him get too close. As long as he remains unavailable he can never get close enough to hurt them.

2. A SUBCONSCIOUS WISH TO BRING DAD BACK HOME

As many already know the relationship one had with their father shapes the relationships they will have with other males. If one grows up without a father or if he was emotionally unavailable, one may find themsekves getting involved with men who act just like their father. Although, they risk getting hurt by being with a bad boy. They might be hoping that if the guy can stick around long enough, eventually he will give you the love you didn't get at home. This is also commonly known as "daddy issues".

3. LOW SELF-ESTEEM

When you feel good about yourself, you set high standards in every area of your life - including your romantic relationships. If a girl is in a relationship with a guy who lies, cheats, talks down to them or mistreats them in any way, then regardless of what they may want others to believe, they do not feel good about themselves. When you value who you are, you treat yourself with high regard and require others to do the same. Treat women with kindness and respect and you'll win in the long run.

CHAPTER SIX

WHY IS SHE TESTING YOU?
IS IT A GAME?

Those few questions, that stubborn attitude, those unexplainable actions... Almost everything a woman does seems to be a test sometimes. Even if she doesn't know it, she is judging your response, and you need to be prepared to have the right answer. First off, it's important to note some of the characteristics that women find attractiv: Confidence, independence, leadership, sense of humor, strength; these are all qualities women find attractive. The reason you need to know this is because when she tests you, she is trying to see if you have these qualities. How you react will determine if you pass the test.

Women instinctively search for a mate with these qualities, among others. So, even if they aren't knowingly trying to test you, they will test their limits and judge your response. For instance, if your girlfriend flirts with other men, she might be trying to see if you will let her get away with it. If you do, you have not shown confidence and leadership. You have shown her that she rules the roost. If she argues with you about where you're going to dinner, she is trying to see if you will take charge and be a leader. If she asks you if you find another girl attractive, she is really testing how you feel about her. Now, there are exceptions to these scenarios, like maybe she's really just flirtacious, or she doesn't like your choice in food, or may want to mimic the fashion style of that girl you were checking out.

From the moment you introduce yourself to a girl, she is testing you. If she makes fun of you for approaching her, she is testing to see if you have the personality to win her over, or if you will just hang your head and walk away. Women want to be with the prize. And the price isn't fazed by little jabs from anyone. If you make a self-defamating joke right back, it shows that you are in control, and you pass the test. Then, when you start dating and she acts like a brat, she is trying to see how much she can get away with. If you let her walk all over you, she knows that you aren't strong enough to take care of her. If she continues, then just leave because odds are she really is just a brat.

Always remember the qualities that a woman finds attractive and gauge your responses to match them. If you do this, your relationships will be much more successful.

Women test men for a lot of reasons, but especially to see how men will react. Keep in mind that attractive women get hit on everyday and they must be able to quickly tell if you're someone who is just a waste of her time or if you're someone who is actually worth her time. Testing a man is a perfect way for a woman to make this distinction and put you in the relationship, fling, or friend category.

Also, women test men to protect themselves from getting hurt. Before giving her heart away to a man, a woman will want to make sure that she will not get her heart broken. So, to prevent herself from getting played, a woman will often try to confuse a man by acting disinterested and making him jealous so as to tell a man that she's not easy and not to be taken advantage of.

HOW DO WOMEN TEST MEN?

SOME COMMON TESTS A WOMAN MAY THROW A MAN'S WAY ARE:

10. Asking you for a subtle favor such as holding her drink

11. Asking you to buy her something such as a drink

12. Asking you crazy dead end questions that don't make sense, such as "Am I fat?"

13. Canceling a date unexpectedly or flaking on you

14. Not calling or texting back

15. Insulting you or making fun of you

16. Giving you an ultimatum

17. Acting 'bitchy' to see if you'll put up with her behavior

18. Flirting with other guys in front of you

19. Teasing you sexually to see what you do

Of course, there are many more ways women test men, but the ones I have listed above almost all men have experienced and can serve as a base for recognizing test patterns.

WHY DO YOU WANT WOMEN TO TEST YOU?

When a woman tests you, it means she's at least mildly attracted to you and trying to find out if she will let herself be more attracted to you on the condition that you pass the tests. Think about it: women don't test guys that they are absolutely not attracted to. Instead, society forces women to act politely and respectfully to men they are not attracted to the likes of how you act towards a cashier at a grocery store. So, if a woman you like is treating you too nice, it's time to ask more questions. If you're passing all of her tests, you're giving yourself a big, big advantage in building more attraction than any other guy that's trying to pursue her. You're separating yourself as the obvious choice for her because you're showing her that no matter what happens, you're still in control of yourself.

WHAT SHOULD YOU DO WHEN YOU'RE BEING TESTED?

Well, there's only one thing you can do - cry. Just kidding. I have found that there's pretty much only a few best ways to deal with a woman's test.

1. NOT PAYING ATTENTION TO THEM

Yes, just ignore them or act like she never said anything. When a woman tests you, she's trying to throw you off balance emotionally. By disregarding or not responding to what she said, you're acting emotionally unaffected by the test and you're not letting yourself fall into the trap.

2. TESTING HER BACK

This is as simple as it sounds. Try throwing one of her tests back at her and see how she reacts to it. By testing her back, you're also telling her indirectly that you're on to her tests and that you speak her lingo.

3. LAUGHING

Lighten up the situation by adding a bit of laughter to it. When you're having fun and enjoying yourself even while she's testing you, she'll know that she's dealing with someone who doesn't take insignificant things so seriously.

CHAPTER SEVEN

THE DO'S AND DON'TS OF THE FIRST DATE

Your first date with someone can make you feel stressed and nervous. Remember, you will never get a second chance to make a first impression, so try to make it a good one. Sometimes it is difficult to figure out what you did on a date that left either a good or not-so-good impression. The following suggestions will offer some beneficial guidelines on what you should or shouldn't do on a first date so you have a better chance at leaving a good impression. Whether or not you ever see this person again is irrelevant, since you should aspire to be remembered as someone that's pleasant to be around, friendly, and a good soul.

Almost all of us want to give our first date a good impression. They say first impression last so make sure you don't mess things up! While you are panicking inside, your date might be trying their best to make everything romantic. Try to focus on your actual date and on the actual conversation that you are going to have while on the date.

Dos:

20. BE YOURSELF: Being yourself is still much better than pretending to be someone you are not.

21. BE A GOOD LISTENER: This date is not just about you. You should know when to listen to your date and stop talking about yourself. This is a getting to know each other date, not a get-to-know-me date.

22. TRY TO HAVE FUN: Be open to new date ideas. Your date night might not be the typical let's go out to dinner and movie afterward. Your date may come up with some cool ideas that make them stand out from the others.

23. CONSIDER WEARING COMFORTABLE SHOES: A long walk in town after dinner or a movie is another way to get to know each other and wearing uncomfortable shoes or clothing may hinder that lovely moment that you're trying to have.

24. MAKE EYE CONTACT: You can tell whether the person is sincere by looking them in the eye or making eye contact. Some can fake it, but it's good to know you that you mean it.

DON'TS:

25. DON'T TALK ABOUT YOUR PAST RELATIONSHIPS: Nobody wants to hear your past relationship on a first date. I mean, that's the reason why you are on a date

right? So forget the past and move on. Try to move on and explore a new horizon.

26. DON'T GET AHEAD OF YOURSELF: Your date may not be the one you are expecting, but give her a chance. Who knows, she may not be expecting you as her date but still may be trying to make a connection.

27. DON'T LEAVE HER HANGING: If you want to see her again on a second date, let her know that the date went great was some positive words like "It was a pleasure meeting you. I had a great time." Sometimes the way you talk to her or your gestures can tell them that you are interested and had fun. On the other hand, if you're not interested, be respectful and courteous at all times.

28. DON'T PRETEND TO BE SOMEONE YOU'RE NOT: If you don't eat shrimp and she loves it, don't eat it just to please her. You may just end up with a rash all over your face and that can turn her off aside from the fact that you are actually trying to please her.

29. DON'T DRINK MORE THAN YOU CAN HANDLE: This is a first date, not a friend that knows the effect of alcohol in your system. A glass of wine or two will do. She may be the right date, but you may turn her off by drinking too much.

30. DON'T TALK DIRTY OR TALK ABOUT SEX: If both of you have planned on having sex then it's probably okay. It's nice

to have a good conversation and that may be something to look forward to on your second date.

31. DON'T TEXT OR TALK ON THE PHONE: Doing this may give your date the impression that you're not interested with the person. When you need to send a very important text or make an important phone call, you can excuse yourself to go the bathroom or something but don't stay there for long either.

32. DO NOT BE LATE: There is no excuse for being late for a first date. If you are late, it had better be because it was a matter of life or death. Being late conveys the idea that you do not respect your date's valuable time and you are unreliable. Punctuality is an admirable and responsible quality.

33. RESPECT HER PERSONAL SPACE: Do not overstep your boundaries by getting too physically close when you talk to your date. This will likely irritate them and make them feel smothered. Back off and show some consideration for their personal space.

CHAPTER EIGHT

CHIVALRY

Dating can sometimes be tiring. It may seem endless. A man may feel that his relationship with a woman is not progressing. When dating seems to have reached a status quo, these dating tips for men could help you push the envelope again and finally make a woman fall for you. Read on this Chivalry tips.

34. SHOW KINDNESS: Most women fall for guys who treat them well (assuming they've got the bad boy stage out of their system). This, however, does not mean that you need to obey her every commands like a dog. There is a huge line between being nice and being a slave. You don't always have to follow what she says; in fact, you are free to say no. You can still treat her right by doing things in her favor. If she wants something, you don't always have to give it to her right away. Sometimes giving it to her when she least expects it can win you extra points. It shows her that you were listening when she may have thought you weren't.

35. LEARN HOW TO FLIRT: Adopt a playful attitude. You will reap good results if you use these dating tips. For men, being playful is a weapon you could use to know if a woman is interested in you. If she responds and flirts back, this means that she likes you. A commonly used technique in flirting includes sending mixed signals. This is where a woman might confuse a man by making you think that they like you and then pulling back as if they are no longer interested.

36. FOCUS ON THE DETAILS: Compliment her hair, her clothes, her bag, her shoes, etc. Women like it when men are able to notice their efforts to look more attractive. If you have not read these dating tips for men, you can easily make mistakes that most men do and become selfish. Try to find something different from her every time you meet. Tell her that her earrings look nice on her and that it fits her dress. Some women don't like too much femminimity, so keep it in check.

37. KNOW WHEN AND WHERE TO TOUCH HER: Increase physical contact as you go on more dates. Be observant of her body language to tell if she likes it or not. If she avoids physical contact, move away and initiate contact again later. If she moves away again, stop. Start by touching the base of her palms, her forearm, and the area above her knees or her elbow as you talk to each other. These areas have many sensitive nerve endings that may trigger sexual arousal. Use slow, graceful, and firm touch. If they are not resceptive, stop.

Lastly, perform acts of chivalry. Women fantasize about romance. They dream of what they read in novels and watch from movies. Acts of chivalry do not mean you need to ride horses and battle other men with swords. It could be simple dating tips such as opening doors for her, holding her arms as she climbs up and down the stairs, or carrying the groceries. All you need to do is show her that you can take good care of her. Use these dating tips to break the status quo in your relationships and finally make the woman you like to fall in love with you.

CHAPTER NINE

HOW DO I KNOW IF SHE LIKES ME?

This can be a big challenge, especially if you are really into her. The last thing you want to do is to go all in only to find out youre' still in The Friend Zone. It happens on both sides. Many of us know that embarrassing scenario and let me tell you it isn't fun. The whole roller coaster of regret can be a real pain in the butt. When you really like her, trying to figure it out seems to become more difficult, mainly because you don't want to screw up.

Who else has trouble figuring out whether or not a woman likes them? This is a huge problem for many guys, and to be honest, it shouldn't be! If a girl really likes you, she will show you in certain ways. If you want to know what those ways are, then continue reading..

Usually, if you have to ask that question, the answer is that she probably does not. Most guys usually look for things that are not really there. So, before I tell you what signs to look for, you need to get outside of your head.

1. LEANING IN

This is one of the most classic signs of interest. If she is leaning into you during your conversation, then she is interested. Just make sure you don't lean in too far; this may convey neediness on your end. With this one, you really need to look at your environment as well. If there is nothing that is making her lean into you, like a crowded bar or overzealous dancing guy behind her, but she does it anyway, then that is a really good sign of interest.

2. SHE FACES YOU COMPLETELY

When a woman is talking to a man she is not interested in, she will never point her body fully in his direction. However, if she is fully facing you, then you can be sure she has at least a slight interest in you or what you're saying. Fully facing someone is referred to as being "locked in" to the conversation.

3. THE SMILE NOD

This one is a really good sign of interest. What you need to look for is a combination of three things. When you are talking to her, she will nod her head slightly in agreement, hold strong eye contact, and smile at you. If she does the "smile, nod" then she is really into you.

4. First off, do not lose sight of our common humanity. Just because she is a woman, do not think she is some alien you'll never understand. That's only half true.. Anyways, she like you

has feelings and wants what's best in her life. If she pays you a lot of compliments, she likes you.

5. When in your company she asks a lot of questions and takes interest in what you do, then she likes you. We as people are very similar in that our actions and behavior change dramatically when we are interested in something. We immediately sit up and pay attention.

6. If you ask her to do something and she drops everything to get it done; in other words, she puts a priority on what you want, she may like you. Additionally, she smiles while in your company and laughs at your ridiculously awful jokes, she likes you. By the way, I am just kidding on that, maybe your jokes are outstanding, but you get what I mean.

Remember, you do not want to be one of the millions of men who completely RUIN their chances with a woman before he even opens his mouth. Research has proven repeatedly that the majority of communication is conveyed through body language. Master the magical art of making her quiver with only your body language...and you will never have to worry about her even thinking about rejecting you.

CHAPTER TEN

BEING SUPPORTIVE AND EXPRESSING FEELINGS

We all want to receive support of some kind - whether spiritual, mental, emotional, physical, or financial. Usually, we expect that support to come from our loved ones, although there are times when we would like it from the rest of the world. In our moments of struggle, we demand it from the Universe. Exactly what is this support that we all crave, and what form should it take in our relationships? Are women and men supposed to give the same kind of support to each other? Or are their differences?

What is the right kind of support? What is a healthy amount that sustains you and still enables you to be independent in the important ways?

All very good questions! And while the answers are usually clear to me, there are times when the dynamics in a particular relationship make the distinctions of what's needed on the part of each person so unclear. So we'll start with the general basis for determining the kind of support that is best given to support your partner in a healthy and balanced relationship. After that, it is up to each of us to delineate the shades of gray that are acceptable to us. I believe that women set the tone for their relationship and can actually create the true foundation for its growth - that is, if they take their responsibility to do so seriously - the most important support that women can provide for men is spiritual and emotional.

Spiritual support is demonstrated through your own connection to the Universe in whatever form works best for you. The idea is that you develop your inner strength through your Soul Self which then manifests through your way of being in the relationship. Your faith is in your Higher Power, your God, your Goddess, your Highest Truth, the Universe, or whatever it may be.. and by showing this in a consistent manner to your partner, you are helping them to develop that trust in the relationship as well. The second means of support for women to provide is emotional support. Now, this doesn't mean you become the mother nurturing your childeren.

Heavens NO! No equality is ever going to come out of that set-up! Rather, once again, you become the role model for Emotional Independence, demonstrating that while you are there to provide him with love, compassion, and understanding, you are not encouraging dependency. Of course, this is your challenge as women to develop this state of Emotional Independence in yourselves. It is a balance of sharing yourself, but yet still relying on yourself to manifest stability. The more you have released that which no longer serves you emotionally, the closer you become to attaining your Emotional Independence. It is necessary for a woman to lay this foundation if there's to be any hope of their partner following the same path.

CHAPTER ELEVEN

HANDLING DISAGREEMENTS
AND ARGUMENTS

Arguments and disagreements are a fact of life. Sometimes they happen because of misunderstandings; sometimes one or both parties are stressed or feeling disrespected; sometimes one person is just plain angry and wants to fight. There are many reasons why this situation occurs and there are different ways of handling it, some better than others. Part of growing up as a well-rounded human being includes learning how to handle disagreements and disputes. Learning about the negative side of life is an important skill to develop and take into adulthood. Certainly, once a child attends school and then college and work, there will, no doubt, be many times when someone is rude, or disagrees or rejects them. Being able to be pragmatic and cope with this situation without being devastated or traumatized by a negative response is vital to a person's emotional mental health and well-being.

Children sense when something is wrong. Part of human survival is based on being sensitive to atmosphere and picking up signals from other people and situations. A large part of communication is done non-verbally, so tension, anger, rage, especially when non-spoken will be picked up at a sensory level by a child. Children tend to think that everything is about them, so if a parent is angry the child will often think that they have done something wrong, even when it is nothing to do with them or their behavior. Why am I talking about children? Because not all of us grow out of this instinctive behavior as quickly as others, and continue to carry it with us throughout adulthood.

This is why it is less unhealthy for a child to see their parents disagreeing in front of them, as opposed to not knowing. It has been found to be more distressing for a child to have their parents split up suddenly, when there has been no indication of problems prior to the split, than if there had been long periods of rows and tensions. Children need to see the whole process of disagreement, from beginning to end. Often parents may decide to put a disagreement to one side, to be continued later. The truth is, it is better for the child to see the whole process, even if both people end up not agreeing. If those people are able to say, 'I do not agree with you, but I respect your point of view and still love you.' then that is a powerful learning experience. Seeing how their parents move through a disagreement process is a very useful lesson in life.

THERE ARE THREE MAIN TYPES OF ARGUMENTS AND DISAGREEMENTS:

Some disagreements can be **constructive**. They clear the air and may well bring previously unspoken resentments out into the open. A constructive disagreement allows for both parties to have their say and be respected and listened to. This then enables the situation to move forward and be resolved.

A **productive** disagreement will bring problems and concerns into the open. This will enable matters to be discussed and each party's point of view to be appreciated. However, this will not necessarily entail a change of either person's mind. Patience and tolerance are important here. These discussions are also respectful and valuable.

Destructive disagreements are where emotions, personal attacks and insults are involved. Often raised voices and tempers are exchanged. These do not tend to resolve problems, but rather refuel them. These situations can fester and cause ongoing tensions, resentments and continual sniping, or maybe the total opposite, where long icy silences occur.

The art of handling an argument or disagreement is in saying, "will this matter in six months time?". Keeping a sense of perspective and a sense of humor enables a more balanced attitude to prevail. This is not the same as being a doormat. It means being assertive enough, but also appreciating that different people may have a different point of view for their own reasons, based on what is happening in their life and what their agenda is. Working through those criteria can facilitate a respectful discussion and a greater understanding. As a final thought, a wise man once said that "the art of negotiation is where each person trades something that they do not mind losing, whilst treating it as if they have made a major concession". This can be a useful thought to bear in mind in these situations.

CHAPTER TWELVE

TIPS AND TRICKS FOR A HEALTHY RELATIONSHIP

Most women aspire to that healthy relationship filled with happiness and joy, with all the roses are red wine, and where the fairytale dream comes true. Relationship challenges represent a crucial key to your love life that cannot and must not be put on hold if you are seeking the happily ever after outcome. The vital step to be taken in order to avoid serious obstacles between you and your partner is to prevent them from coming up and becoming a destabilizing issue.

One way of preventing unwanted problems is to have a sentimental bond based on strong communication.

The old saying "Communication is key!" is entirely true and it works great for our modern day couples who tend to forget the importance of sharing meaningful thoughts and feelings. Relationship challenges occur when partners forget to express themselves freely and talk about what is going on in their lives. So, what you need to do is help your relationship grow by letting your partner know you inside and out.

Honesty and trust derive from consolidating communication within the couple. Establishing trust on all levels is a two-way road that is bound to take you to the place you have always dreamed of. Mutual trust guarantees loyalty and respect which are part of the foundation of every healthy relationship. It relies on the concept that we have to respect the fact that each one of us is different and instead of fighting against them, one should learn to love them.

Whenever partners fail to choose an appropriate approach to the situation, relationship challenges intervene, such as pressuring the other to do things they do not want to do or abusing them on various levels. Learn to be there for one and other unconditionally. Even though you had a fight, if your lover needs your support, you should be able to provide it no matter what. Give your partner some space if that is what he or shes need, but be sure to offer comfort and a shoulder to cry on when they decide to open up to you.

This is the special ingredient that makes the recipe for an ideal love bond, as most relationship challenges can be overcome once both partners are aware that the person sitting next to them in this incredible journey supports them every step of the way. Despite the fact that couples try to keep the fire burning, there may be moments when the intensity of your feelings tend to fade away and the focus point of your love life and interests shift in a selfish way. Don't forget to show affection every once in a while; go down memory lane and try to feel and visualize that perfect moment when you two first met.

These tips should do the trick and prevent relationship challenges of standing in the way of your happy ending. Fairy tales do come true as long as the characters of each love story decide to write the pages themselves.

TIPS AND TRICKS TO TURN AN UNHEALTHY RELATIONSHIP INTO A HEALTHY RELATIONSHIP

1. STOP REHASHING THE PAST.

It's important to discuss the issues in your relationship, but that doesn't mean bringing up the past in every argument. In order to grow as a couple, especially after a breakup or a communication breakdown, you must forgive each other. Of course, forgiveness doesn't come easily; you must decide, once and for all, whether to let the past go or let the relationship go. If you spent any time broken up with your partner, you know how hard it is to be apart. So, prepare to move forward. That means, no more trying to make your partner feel guilty about past mistakes. Don't bring up the past when having a disagreement about the present, and don't use the past to justify your current feelings or behaviors. There's no way to turn an unhealthy relationship into a healthy relationship while holding on to old resentments. The festering anger and constant rehashing of the past will lead to bitterness, bad arguments, and a dismal future. Don't let the past ruin your future. You can create new, better memories together, but only if both partners willingly forgive the past.

2. DEAL WITH THE REAL RELATIONSHIP ISSUES.

Forgiving the past does not mean ignoring relationship issues. Unhealthy relationships often come from inattention to underlying problems. In the past, you may have argued over everything without really fixing anything. Or, you may have dealt with the symptoms of relationship issues rather than digging up the root cause.

For example, if everything blew up after one of you was unfaithful, the focus may land squarely on that single act of betrayal. Cheating is horrible and inexcusable, but there is almost always a problem beneath the surface. Were you feeling vengeful, unfulfilled, or insecure? Did your partner feel ignored, unloved, or neglected? Had your relationship become too mundane or boring? Did you miscommunicate your desires? Is your partner not ready for total commitment? Sometimes it is difficult for couples to discover all the underlying issues, so don't hesitate to bring in a neutral third party. This might mean going to couples counseling or using online relationship repair sources.

Once you understand the root cause, you can clearly see if it is fixable. If so, develop a solid plan to prevent breakup and breakdown of your love. Make sure you both agree on this solution, since it takes two committed partners to turn an unhealthy relationship into a healthy one again.

3. GIVE YOUR ALL. DON'T HOLD BACK.

Some couples feel insecure when rekindling love after a break up or break down. It's tempting to hold back, just in case things go wrong again. However, this approach sets you up for failure. Try to find comfort in the fact that your partner chose to work things out with you, even though it might be easier to give up on the unhealthy relationship.

Many couples just break up rather than fix a broken relationship. Instead, you're working to build a healthy relationship. That's what makes your love special. Use this knowledge to bolster feelings of security so you can give your all in the relationship. Don't hold back out of fear or distrust. Don't put your love on probation while you wait for something else to go wrong.

Set your mind on healing the relationship rift, loving each other more completely, and creating happy memories together. You wouldn't take the time to read about how to turn an unhealthy relationship into a healthy relationship if you didn't love your partner enough to try. When relationship issues arise (and they will), remember that it takes more work to stay in love than to fall in love. Also, remember that it is worth it. True love lasts because two people refuse to give up on a love that's worth fighting for. If it starts to get really bad, ask yourself "How would I feel telling friends and family that *this* is the reason we broke up?". If it sounds minisule, it probably is. Best wishes and a happy relationship to you.

CONCLUSION

Women don't really make much sense to men. Most men are unable to understand or comprehend why women behave the way they do. It just doesn't make any logical sense. But then again, neither do men (to women). The reason for this is that both men and women have a totally different set of needs. That's why most of the things that seem to work don't really make much sense at all.

Do you have trouble understanding women in relationships? Does it sometimes feel like women are complex puzzles that even the wisest men can fail to figure out? Maintaining good relationships with women is really less complex than you think.

Women crave the drama. Then again, so do men. They need your utmost undivided attention; they want to feel loved; they want you to tell them they're beautiful and they never seem to be content no matter how hard you try. Reassurance, understanding, and lots of cuddles, my friend; these three can work wonders. Make sure to constantly communicate with your girl so you can both address the issues or problems right away, and together, come up with a solution. Remember that you're a team and always make it a point to express your love to each other. Fights and misunderstandings are normal. It's a part of your growth. It can sometimes even be healthy. So, enjoy the moment, learn from mistakes and continue the romance.

How often have you found yourself confused over the subject of women? How often do you find yourself trying to figure out why women do what they do and what the primary motive behind most of their actions is? If you are like most guys out there, I am pretty sure that you've at some point found yourself confused when trying to figure women out. But don't worry... Follow these useful tips and you'll finally understand why women are the way they are. Wishing everyone the happiest of relationships and love!

Again, please feel free to check some of my other work, including How to Understand Men if you're curious as to why he does some of the things he does!

Manufactured by Amazon.ca
Bolton, ON